Today's Girl

SAY NO TO CHILD MARRIAGE

By Dr Rumbidzai Nyanhoto

Illustrated by N.Yaseen

ISBN: 978-0-6453448-2-0

Dedication

In memory of all the children who lost their lives as a result of child marriage, may their souls rest in peace.

This book is dedicated to every girl who faces the reality of child marriage. Always remember you are special, your life has meaning, and your dreams matter. You have the power to grow into a strong and successful woman.

This book is written to guide you, encourage you, and help you find the courage to say NO to child marriage.

"Our children are our greatest treasure. They are our future. Those who abuse them tear at the fabric of our society and weaken our nation." - Nelson Mandela

WHO IS A CHILD?

A child is any person under the age of eighteen.

WHAT DOES IT MEAN TO BE A CHILD?

- Children require adults to care for them; they are not yet mature enough to provide care for themselves or other people around them because of their age.

- Because of their age, children cannot protect themselves from any danger; they require their parents and adults around them to provide protection. Childrens' bodies are still developing; therefore, they still require time to mature to engage in things done by adult bodies.

WHAT IS CHILD MARRIAGE?

Child marriage is any marriage or union between a child under 18 and an adult or another child.

WHY DOES CHILD MARRIAGE HAPPEN?

Poverty:

Some families marry off their daughters because they hope to get money, animals, or gifts (called a dowry or bride price) to help the family survive. Others do it to build or keep close ties with wealthy families, hoping those families will support them in times of need.

Culture and Customs:

In some places, people believe child marriage keeps traditions alive, but not all traditions are good. In some cultures, when adults in the family commit crimes that lead to loss of life in the community, girls are exchanged as compensation or to calm the spirits.

Religion:

Religion is a belief in God, gods or spiritual beings. Sometimes, child marriage is wrongly linked to religion. In some cases, religious leaders who force children into marriage claim to hear messages from god or advise that the spirits inspire their actions. But a loving God or spirit does not want to harm children.

CONSEQUENCES - WHY SHOULD I SAY NO TO CHILD MARRIAGE?

Child marriage is against my rights. It takes away my right to be protected.

Child marriage forces me to become a mother before I am ready. I need time to grow, learn, and enjoy being a child first.

Child marriage is not love. It is rape, it is sexual violence, and it is against the law.

My body is not ready for pregnancy. If I am forced to give birth too soon, I could get very sick or even die. Even the baby may not survive.

Child marriage forces me to leave school. It shatters my dreams and takes away my chance to build a successful future and career.

If I don't say NO to child marriage, the cycle will continue—more girls will face pain, abuse, and even death. By standing up, I help protect myself and other girls too.

HOW CAN I SAY NO

Believe in yourself first - Saying NO starts with believing in yourself. Before you talk to anyone else, tell yourself: "I am special. I deserve a better future. I have the right to be safe."
Be confident and strong in your decision, because saying NO to child marriage is the right choice for you and your future

Decide early - Waiting until the marriage day to say NO can be very hard and unsafe. It's better to ask for help early. Ask for help as soon as possible.

Stay safe - Don't try to stop it alone; it can be dangerous. Talk to someone you can trust. You can speak to professionals like:
- A teacher
- A social worker
- A counsellor or health worker

Do not share your plans with the people forcing you into marriage; they may try to stop you from getting help.

QUESTIONS YOU MIGHT HAVE

What if it's my religion? Won't saying NO be a punishable sin by the spirits or God?

Whatever God or spiritual being people believe in is expected to protect them, right? Why would anyone believe in a God or spirit that wants to harm people? Why would anyone follow a religion that hurts only girls and not boys? Something is not adding up. Never agree to child marriage because of religion.

But this has been our custom or tradition from our forefathers. How can I be the one to break it?

People create culture and traditions—they are not unchangeable. Good traditions protect people and help them live better lives. If a tradition forces you into child marriage, then it is not a good tradition. You have the right to choose what works for you.

I am worried that if I say NO? my parents' expectations will be shattered. They will hate me, and it will destroy our relationship.

Parents are responsible for working hard to feed and care for their families. If they struggle, child marriage should not be the answer. Why should your life and future be the price? Real love does not hurt. If your parents truly love you, they will not treat you like an object or a source of wealth. They should not force you into marriage for their own gain.

Toy

I'm worried that if I report him, he will go to prison.

Prisons exist for a reason. They correct people who break the law and protect others from harm. Trust the law to guide people's behaviour and to keep society safe.

What if I want to say NO, but I'm scared?

You are not alone. There are always people who can help you. Talk to a professional you trust, such as a teacher, social worker, or child protection worker.

What if I've already agreed but don't want any more?

It is never too late to say NO. Marriage is a lifetime commitment, which means it will affect your whole life. You do not want to live in regret. Reach out to a trusted professional near you today—they can help you.

SAYING NO ISN'T EASY BUT WORTH IT.

UNITED NATIONS – CONVENTION ON THE RIGHTS OF THE CHILD

Did you know?

A long time ago, in 1989, leaders from many countries came together and made a very important promise to all the children in the world.

They created something called the United Nations Convention on the Rights of the Child. That's a big name, but it simply means an international agreement to protect childhood.

This agreement is the most widely accepted human rights promise in history. Since then, it has helped change and improve the lives of millions of children all around the world.

Let's look at some of the rights that protect children from child marriage.

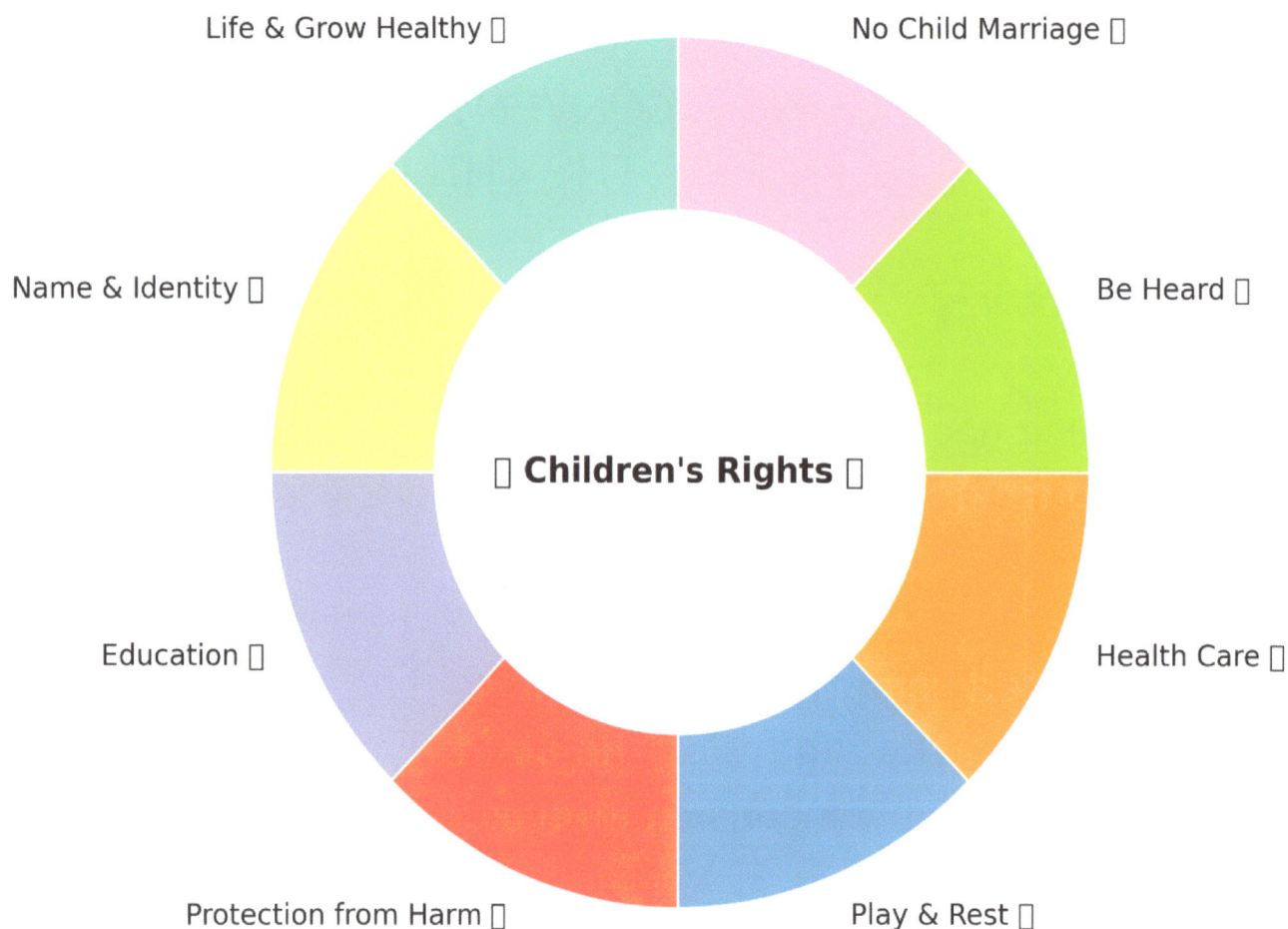

Life & Grow Healthy

No Child Marriage

Name & Identity

Be Heard

Children's Rights

Education

Health Care

Protection from Harm

Play & Rest

When you say NO to child marriage, you are joining hands with leaders all around the world who have promised to protect children's rights.

About the author

Hello! My name is Dr. Rumbidzai Nyanhoto, but you can call me Dr. Rumbi.

I am a teacher, writer, and social worker who works with children and families. In my work, I meet many children who face difficult challenges, but I also see how strong and brave they can be. I also faced a few challenges when I was a child, but I overcame them. I hope to share my story with you one day. I want you to know that whatever challenges you face, you too can rise above them.

I wrote this book because I believe every child deserves to be safe, loved, and free to dream big. I want you to know that you are important, your voice matters, and your future is bright.

Always remember: **You have the right to say NO to child marriage and YES to your dreams!**

www.ingramcontent.com/pod-product-compliance
Lightning Source LLC
LaVergne TN
LVHW072125070426
835511LV00003B/94